¡A jugar! / Ways to Play

¡A JUGAR EN CASA!
WE PLAY WITH THINGS AROUND THE HOUSE!

By Leonard Atlantic
traducido por / translated by Eida de la Vega

Gareth Stevens
PUBLISHING

Please visit our website, www.garethstevens.com. For a free color catalog of all our high-quality books, call toll free 1-800-542-2595 or fax 1-877-542-2596.

Cataloging-in-Publication Data

Names: Atlantic, Leonard.
Title: We play with things around the house! = ¡A jugar en casa! / Leonard Atlantic.
Description: New York : Gareth Stevens Publishing, 2018. | Series: Ways to play = ¡A jugar! | In English and Spanish | Includes index.
Identifiers: ISBN 9781538205785 (library bound)
Subjects: LCSH: Play–Juvenile literature. | Games–Juvenile literature.
Classification: LCC HQ782.A43 2018 | DDC 790–dc23

Published in 2018 by
Gareth Stevens Publishing
111 East 14th Street, Suite 349
New York, NY 10003

Translator: Eida de la Vega
Editorial Director, Spanish: Nathalie Beullens-Maoui
Editor: Ryan Nagelhout
Designer: Bethany Perl

Photo credits: Cover, p. 1 Dima Sidelnikov/Shutterstock.com; p. 5 wavebreakmedia/Shutterstock.com; p. 7 Rawpixel.com/Shutterstock.com; p. 9 Mieke Dalle/Photographer's Choice/Getty Images; p. 11 FatCamera/E+/Getty Images; p. 13, 15 (background), (boy) Africa Studio/Shutterstock.com; p. 17 JGI/Jamie Grill/Blend Images/Getty Images; p. 19 Jamie Grill/Tetra Images/Getty Images; p. 21 VGstockstudio/Shutterstock.com; p. 23 espies/Shutterstock.com.

Printed in the United States of America

CPSIA compliance information: Batch #CS17GS: For further information contact Gareth Stevens, New York, New York at 1-800-542-2595.

Contenido

Contents

Puedes jugar en cualquier lugar. ¡Incluso dentro de la casa!

....

You can play anywhere. You can even play in the house!

¡Jugamos a las escondidas!

We play hide and seek!

Billy se esconde bajo la cama.

Billy hides under the bed.

A Anthony le gusta
el juego de pillar.

Anthony likes
to play tag.

Molly juega con cajas.

Molly plays with boxes.

Puedes hacer un auto.

You can make a car.

La mamá de Mary pone música. ¡Vamos a bailar!

....

Mary's mom
puts on music.
We have a dance party!

Puedes usar almohadas
para hacer una casa.

....

You can use pillows
to make a house.

Puedes hacer volar un avión. Los hacemos de papel.

....

You can fly a plane. We make them out of paper.

Yo hago el mío con
papel rojo.

....

I make mine
with red paper.

Palabras que debes aprender
Words to Know

(la) cama
bed

(la) almohada
pillow

Índice / Index